QUICK & EASY
PIZZAS

Consultant Editor:
Valerie Ferguson

HERMES
HOUSE

Contents

Introduction

The pizza is the world's favourite fast food – a crisp, golden crust topped with melted cheese, tomatoes and almost any other savoury ingredient from artichokes to ham and from smoked salmon to spinach. It originated in Naples as a simple and inexpensive snack that was easy to eat with the fingers and has never looked back since leaving its native city.

This book includes recipes for basic dough, a super-fast version for those in a hurry and a fail-safe method with a food processor. Nowadays, too, it is possible to buy fresh, frozen or long-life pizza bases from most supermarkets. Although they never taste quite as good as the home-made variety, they can be very useful to keep on hand.

As for toppings – the choice is virtually limitless. You can include or omit almost anything you like – from extra pepperoni to no cheese. The recipes in this book range from classics to substantial meaty meals and from fish and seafood to vegetarian. As well as being a convenient snack, the pizza, perhaps served with a salad, makes a filling lunch or supper dish. Little pizzettes and thin wedges of pizza also make stylish starters and wonderful party food.

Ingredients

A range of fresh and store cupboard ingredients and a selection of herbs and spices will enable you to make pizzas with flair and flavour.

Olive Oil: Used for making the base, brushing, pre-cooking toppings and for drizzling over the finished pizza. A good olive oil is essential. It may be flavoured with herbs and spices.

Herbs & Spices: Fresh herbs are best. Basil has an affinity with tomatoes. Parsley and thyme are "all-purpose" herbs, and chives give a hint of onion. Oregano features widely in Italian cuisine. Sage, which has a strong flavour, is also used.

Chillies are essential for hot and spicy pizzas. Salt and black pepper bring out the full flavour of other ingredients. Other useful spices include ground cumin and grated nutmeg.

Cheeses: Mozzarella, with its stretchy melting quality, is a popular choice for pizzas. Ricotta is used for its mild flavour, and Gruyère, dolcelatte, feta, goat's cheese, Pecorino and Parmesan provide flavours that contrast well with fresh vegetables.

Fish & Seafood:
Prawns, mussels, squid and salmon make delicious toppings. Canned fish, such as tuna and anchovies are traditional and very convenient.

Prawns

Poultry & Fresh Meat: Chicken – both fresh and smoked – is versatile. Lean minced beef cooks quickly and is easy to arrange evenly over the pizza.

Cured Meats: Traditional toppings include spicy sausages, such as pepperoni, prosciutto and other kinds of ham and a range of sliced meats. Most of these are available from larger supermarkets.

Vegetables: Used on their own or with meat or fish, fresh vegetables are essential. Cultivated and wild mushrooms make wonderful toppings. Tomatoes, sliced or made into a sauce, are indispensable. Peppers add colour and flavour.

Peppers

Store Cupboard Ingredients: Olives and capers are traditional toppings and add piquancy. Sun-dried tomatoes have a concentrated flavour, and the oil may also be used for cooking. Tomato purée and sun-dried tomato paste enrich sauces and toppings. Tapenade, a French olive paste, and pesto, an Italian herb sauce, may be used in the same way. Pine nuts add texture and extra flavour.

Olives

Basic Recipes

Basic Pizza Dough

This simple bread base is rolled out thinly for a traditional pizza recipe.

Makes
1 x 25–30 cm/10–12 in round pizza base
4 x 13 cm/5 in round pizza bases
1 x 30 x 18 cm/12 x 7 in rectangular pizza base

INGREDIENTS
175 g/6 oz/1½ cups strong
    white flour
1.5 ml/¼ tsp salt
5 ml/1 tsp easy-blend
    dried yeast
120–150 ml/4–5 fl oz/½–⅔ cup
    lukewarm water
15 ml/1 tbsp olive oil

1 Sift the flour and salt into a large mixing bowl. Stir in the yeast. Make a well in the centre of the dry ingredients. Pour in the water and oil and mix with a spoon to a soft dough.

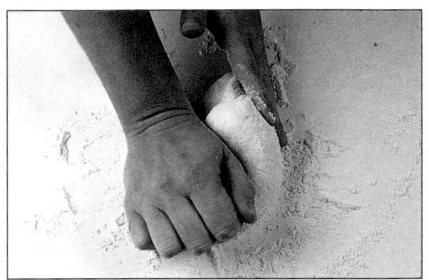

2 Knead the dough on a lightly floured surface for about 10 minutes until smooth and elastic.

3 Place the dough in a greased bowl, and cover with clear film. Leave in a warm place to rise for about 1 hour, or until the dough has doubled in size.

4 Knock back the dough. Turn on to a lightly floured surface, and knead again for 2–3 minutes. Roll out as required and place on a greased baking sheet. Push up the dough to make a rim. The dough is now ready for your choice of topping.

Using a Food Processor

For speed make the pizza dough in a food processor.

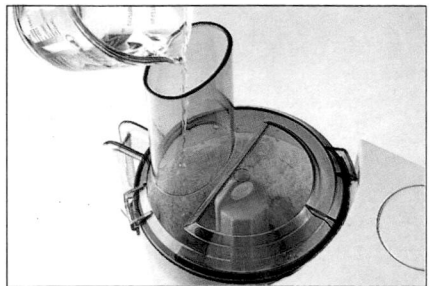

1 Put the flour, salt and yeast into a food processor. Process to mix. Measure the water and add the oil. With the machine running, add the liquid and process until the dough forms a soft ball. Leave to rest for 2 minutes, then process for 1 minute more to knead.

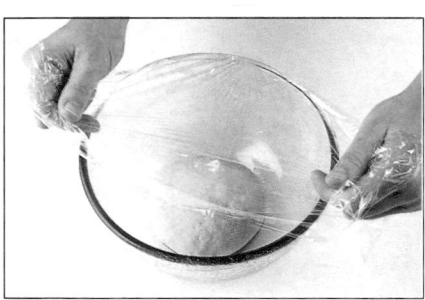

2 Remove the dough from the processor and shape into a neat round. Place in a greased bowl and cover with clear film. Leave in a warm place for about 1 hour until doubled in size. Knock back and knead the dough for 2–3 minutes. The dough is now ready to use.

Superquick Pizza Dough

If you're really pressed for time, try a packet pizza dough mix.

Makes
1 x 25–30 cm/10–12 in round pizza base
4 x 13 cm/5 in round pizza bases
1 x 30 x 18 cm/12 x 7 in rectangular pizza base

INGREDIENTS
1 x 150 g/5 oz packet pizza
base mix
120 ml/4 fl oz/½ cup
lukewarm water

1 Empty the contents of the packet into a mixing bowl. Pour in the water and mix with a wooden spoon to a soft dough.

2 Turn the dough on to a lightly floured surface and knead for 5 minutes until smooth and elastic. The dough is now ready to use.

Tomato Sauce

Many of the recipes use tomato sauce as the basis of the topping on pizzas.

Covers
1 x 25–30 cm/10–12 in round pizza base
1 x 30 x 18 cm/12 x 7 in rectangular pizza base

INGREDIENTS
15 ml/1 tbsp olive oil
1 onion, finely chopped
1 garlic clove, crushed
400 g/14 oz can chopped tomatoes
15 ml/1 tbsp tomato purée
15 ml/1 tbsp chopped fresh mixed herbs,
    such as parsley, thyme, basil and oregano
pinch of sugar
salt and freshly ground black pepper

1 Heat the oil in a pan and fry the onion and garlic until softened. Add the tomatoes, tomato purée, herbs, sugar and seasoning.

2 Simmer, stirring occasionally, for about 45 minutes, or until the tomatoes have reduced to a thick pulp.

Flavoured Oils

For extra flavour brush these over the pizza base before adding the topping. They also form a kind of protective seal that keeps the crust crisp and dry.

Chilli

INGREDIENTS
150 ml/¼ pint/⅔ cup olive oil
10 ml/2 tsp tomato purée
15 ml/1 tbsp dried red chilli flakes

1 Heat the oil in a pan until very hot but not smoking. Stir in the tomato purée and red chilli flakes. Leave to cool. Pour the chilli oil into a small jar or bottle. Cover and store in the fridge for up to 2 months.

Garlic

INGREDIENTS
3–4 garlic cloves
120 ml/4 fl oz/½ cup olive oil

1 Peel the garlic cloves and put them into a jar or bottle. Pour in the oil, cover and refrigerate for up to 1 month.

Margherita

This classic pizza is simple to prepare. The sweet flavour of sun-ripe tomatoes works wonderfully with the basil and Mozzarella.

Serves 2–3

INGREDIENTS
1 pizza base, 25–30 cm/
   10–12 in diameter
30 ml/2 tbsp olive oil
1 quantity Tomato Sauce
150 g/5 oz Mozzarella cheese
2 ripe tomatoes, thinly sliced
6–8 fresh basil leaves
30 ml/2 tbsp freshly grated
   Parmesan cheese
freshly ground black pepper

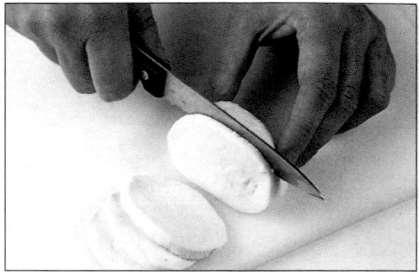

2 With a sharp knife, cut the Mozzarella cheese into thin slices.

3 Arrange the sliced Mozzarella and tomatoes on top of the pizza base in overlapping circles.

1 Preheat the oven to 220°C/425°F/ Gas 7. Brush the pizza base with 15 ml/1 tbsp of the oil and then spread over the tomato sauce.

COOK'S TIP: If available, try to use real Italian buffalo Mozzarella cheese. The flavour is much better than other types.

VARIATIONS: As with many tomato-based toppings, anchovies and/or capers can make an interesting addition.

You could also add a variety of thinly sliced vegetables, such as courgettes, slices of ham or sausage, nuts or flaked tuna, to this basic pizza before adding the cheese.

4 Roughly tear the basil leaves, and scatter them over the pizza. Sprinkle with the Parmesan. Drizzle over the remaining oil and season with black pepper. Bake for 15–20 minutes, until crisp and golden. Serve immediately.

Marinara

The combination of garlic, good quality olive oil and oregano give this pizza an unmistakably Italian flavour.

Serves 2–3

INGREDIENTS
60 ml/4 tbsp olive oil
675 g/1½ lb plum tomatoes, peeled, seeded
 and chopped
1 pizza base, 25–30 cm/
 10–12 in diameter
4 garlic cloves, cut into slivers
15 ml/1 tbsp chopped
 fresh oregano
salt and freshly ground
 black pepper

1 Preheat the oven to 220°C/425°F/ Gas 7. Heat 30 ml/2 tbsp of the oil in a pan. Add the tomatoes and cook, stirring frequently, for about 5 minutes, until soft.

2 Place the tomatoes in a sieve and leave to drain for about 5 minutes.

3 Transfer the tomatoes to a food processor or blender and process until a smooth purée.

4 Brush the pizza base with half the remaining oil. Spoon over the tomatoes and sprinkle with garlic and oregano. Drizzle over the remaining oil and season with salt and pepper. Bake for 15–20 minutes, until crisp and golden. Serve immediately.

VARIATION: The garlic flavour can be made milder by blanching the whole cloves in boiling water for 2 minutes before slicing.

Quattro Formaggi

Topped with four cheeses, these individual pizzas are quick to assemble, and the aroma, while they are cooking, is irresistible. They make a delicious light lunch, served with a crisp green salad.

Serves 4

INGREDIENTS
4 x 13 cm/5 in round
    pizza bases
15 ml/1 tbsp Garlic Oil
½ small red onion, very
    thinly sliced
50 g/2 oz dolcelatte cheese
50 g/2 oz Mozzarella cheese
50 g/2 oz/½ cup grated
    Gruyère cheese
30 ml/2 tbsp freshly grated
    Parmesan cheese
15 ml/1 tbsp chopped
    fresh thyme
freshly ground black pepper

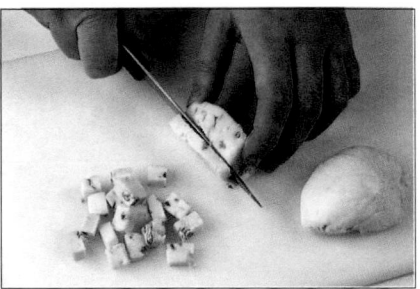

2 Cut the dolcelatte and Mozzarella into cubes and scatter over the bases.

3 Mix together the Gruyère, Parmesan and thyme and sprinkle over the top.

VARIATION: A mature Farmhouse Cheddar is a good substitute if Gruyère cheese is not available.

1 Preheat the oven to 220°C/425°F/ Gas 7. Place the pizza bases well apart on two greased baking sheets, then push up the dough edges to make a thin rim. Brush with garlic oil and top with the red onion.

4 Grind over plenty of black pepper. Bake for 15–20 minutes, until crisp and golden and the cheese is bubbling. Serve immediately.

Fiorentina

Spinach is the star ingredient of this pizza. A grating of nutmeg to heighten its flavour gives this pizza its unique character.

Serves 2–3

INGREDIENTS
175 g/6 oz spinach
45 ml/3 tbsp olive oil
1 small red onion, thinly sliced
1 pizza base, 25–30 cm/
 10–12 in diameter
1 quantity Tomato Sauce
freshly grated nutmeg
150 g/5 oz Mozzarella cheese
1 egg
25 g/1 oz/¼ cup grated
 Gruyère cheese

1 Preheat the oven to 220°C/425°F/ Gas 7. Remove and discard the spinach stalks and wash the leaves in plenty of cold water. Drain well and pat dry with kitchen paper.

2 Heat 15 ml/1 tbsp of the olive oil and fry the sliced red onion for about 5 minutes until soft. Add the spinach and continue to fry until just wilted. Drain off any excess liquid.

3 Brush the pizza base with half the remaining oil. Spread over the tomato sauce, then top with the spinach mixture. Grate over some nutmeg.

4 Thinly slice the Mozzarella and arrange over the spinach. Drizzle over the remaining oil. Bake for 10 minutes, then remove from the oven.

VARIATION: Frozen spinach can be used, but be sure that it is properly thawed and thoroughly drained before using.

5 Make a small well in the centre and drop the egg into the hole.

6 Sprinkle over the grated Gruyère cheese and return to the oven for a further 5–10 minutes, until crisp and golden. Serve immediately.

Quattro Stagioni

The topping on this pizza is divided into four quarters, one for each season of the year. You may substitute any other seasonal favourites.

Serves 4

INGREDIENTS
450 g/1 lb peeled plum tomatoes,
    fresh or canned, weighed whole,
    without extra juice
75 ml/5 tbsp olive oil
115 g/4 oz/1½ cups thinly
    sliced mushrooms
1 garlic clove, finely chopped
4 pizza bases, 20 cm/8 in diameter
350 g/12 oz/3 cups Mozzarella cheese,
    cut into small dice
4 thin slices of cooked ham, cut into
    5 cm/2 in squares
32 black olives, stoned and halved
8 artichoke hearts preserved in oil,
    drained and cut in half
5 ml/1 tsp fresh oregano leaves
salt and freshly ground
    black pepper

1 Preheat the oven to 220°C/425°F/ Gas 7. Strain the tomatoes through the medium holes of a food mill placed over a bowl, scraping in all the pulp.

2 Heat 30 ml/2 tbsp of the oil and lightly sauté the mushrooms. Stir in the garlic and set aside.

3 Spread the puréed tomato on the prepared pizza dough, leaving the rim uncovered. Sprinkle evenly with the Mozzarella. Spread mushrooms over one quarter of the pizza.

4 Arrange the ham on another quarter, and the olives and artichoke hearts on the two remaining quarters. Sprinkle with oregano and the remaining olive oil and season to taste. Bake for about 15–20 minutes, or until the crust is golden brown.

Salmon & Avocado

Smoked and fresh salmon, mixed with avocado, make a delicious topping. Try using smoked salmon trimmings which are cheaper than slices.

Serves 3–4

INGREDIENTS
150 g/5 oz salmon fillet
120 ml/4 fl oz/½ cup dry white wine
1 pizza base, 25–30 cm/10–12 in diameter
15 ml/1 tbsp olive oil
400 g/14 oz can chopped tomatoes,
    drained well
115 g/4 oz/1 cup grated Mozzarella cheese
1 small avocado
10 ml/2 tsp lemon juice
30 ml/2 tbsp crème fraîche
75 g/3 oz smoked salmon, cut into strips
15 ml/1 tbsp capers, drained
30 ml/2 tbsp snipped fresh chives, to garnish
freshly ground black pepper

1 Preheat the oven to 220°C/425°F/ Gas 7. Place the salmon fillet in a frying pan, pour over the wine and season with pepper. Bring to the boil over a low heat, remove from the heat, cover and cool. (The fish will continue to cook.) Skin and flake the salmon into small pieces, removing any bones.

2 Brush the pizza base with the oil and spread over the drained tomatoes. Sprinkle over 50 g/2 oz/½ cup of the Mozzarella. Bake for 10 minutes, then remove from the oven.

3 Meanwhile, halve, stone and peel the avocado. Cut the flesh into small cubes and toss in the lemon juice.

4 Dot teaspoonsful of the crème fraîche over the pizza base.

5 Arrange the fresh and smoked salmon, avocado, capers and remaining grated Mozzarella on top. Season with freshly ground black pepper. Bake for a further 5–10 minutes, until crisp and golden.

6 Sprinkle over the chives to garnish and serve the pizza immediately.

Tuna, Anchovy & Caper

This pizza makes a substantial supper dish, which will provide two to three generous portions when accompanied by a simple salad.

Serves 2–3

INGREDIENTS
30 ml/2 tbsp olive oil
1 quantity Tomato Sauce
1 small red onion
200 g/7 oz can tuna in brine, drained
15 ml/1 tbsp capers, drained
12 stoned black olives
45 ml/3 tbsp freshly grated
   Parmesan cheese
50 g/2 oz can anchovy fillets, drained
   and halved lengthways
freshly ground black pepper

FOR THE SCONE PIZZA DOUGH
115 g/4 oz/1 cup self-raising flour
115 g/4 oz/1 cup self-raising
   wholemeal flour
pinch of salt
50 g/2 oz/4 tbsp butter, diced
about 150 ml/¼ pint/⅔ cup milk

1 Mix together the flours and salt in a bowl. Add the diced butter and rub in until the mixture resembles fine breadcrumbs. Add the milk and mix to a soft dough with a wooden spoon. Turn out on to a lightly floured surface and knead lightly until smooth.

2 Preheat the oven to 220°C/425°F/ Gas 7. Roll out the dough on a lightly floured surface to a 25 cm/10 in circle. Place on a greased baking sheet and brush with 15 ml/1 tbsp of the oil. Spread the tomato sauce evenly over the dough.

3 Cut the onion into thin wedges and arrange on top. Roughly flake the drained tuna with a fork and scatter over the onion.

4 Sprinkle over the capers, black olives and Parmesan. Lattice the anchovy fillets to make a pattern over the top of the pizza.

5 Drizzle over the remaining oil, then grind over plenty of black pepper. Bake for 5–10 minutes, until crisp and golden. Serve immediately.

Anchovy, Pepper & Tomato

This pretty, summery pizza is utterly simple, yet quite delicious. It's well worth grilling the peppers as they take on a lovely smoky flavour.

Serves 2–3

INGREDIENTS
6 plum tomatoes
45 ml/3 tbsp olive oil
5 ml/1 tsp salt
1 large red pepper
1 large yellow pepper
1 pizza base, 25–30 cm/10–12 in diameter
2 garlic cloves, chopped
50 g/2 oz can anchovy
    fillets, drained
freshly ground black pepper
fresh basil leaves,
    to garnish

2 Meanwhile, preheat the oven to 220°C/425°F/Gas 7. Slice the peppers in half lengthways and remove the seeds. Place the pepper halves, skin-side up, on a baking sheet and grill until the skins are evenly charred.

1 Halve the tomatoes lengthways and scoop out the seeds with a small spoon. Roughly chop the flesh and place in a bowl with 15 ml/1 tbsp of the oil and the salt. Mix well, then leave to marinate for 30 minutes.

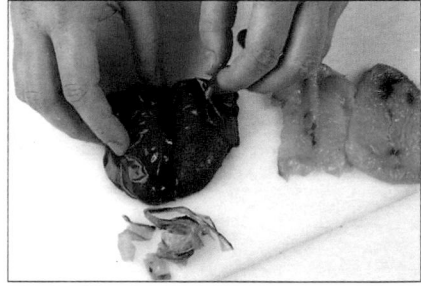

3 Place the peppers in a covered bowl for 10 minutes, then peel off the skins. Cut the flesh into thin strips.

4 Brush the pizza base with half the remaining oil. Drain the tomatoes, then scatter over the base with the peppers and garlic.

5 Snip over the anchovy fillets and season with pepper. Drizzle over the remaining oil and bake for 15–20 minutes, until the base is crisp and golden. Garnish with basil leaves and serve immediately.

Seafood

Almost any combination of your favourite shellfish or other seafood can be used as a pizza topping.

Serves 3–4

INGREDIENTS
450 g/1 lb peeled plum tomatoes,
   fresh or canned, weighed whole,
   without extra juice
175 g/6 oz small squid
225 g/8 oz fresh mussels
1 pizza base, 25–30 cm/10–12 in diameter
175 g/6 oz prawns, raw or cooked, peeled
   and deveined
2 garlic cloves, finely chopped
45 ml/3 tbsp chopped fresh parsley
salt and freshly ground black pepper
45 ml/3 tbsp olive oil

1 Preheat the oven to 220°C/425°F/ Gas 7. Strain the tomatoes through the medium holes of a food mill placed over a bowl, scraping in all the pulp.

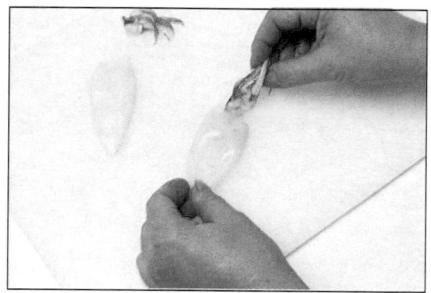

2 Clean the squid by first peeling off the thin skin from the body. Rinse well. Pull the head and tentacles away from the sac. Some of the intestines will come away with the head.

3 Remove and discard the quill and any remaining insides from the sac. Sever the tentacles from the head. Discard the head and intestines. Remove the small hard beak from the base of the tentacles. Rinse the sac and tentacles under running water. Drain. Slice the sacs into thin rings 5 mm/ ¼ in thick.

4 Scrape the beard and any barnacles off the mussels and scrub well. Rinse in cold water. Discard any that are open or have broken shells. Place the mussels in a saucepan and heat until they open. Lift them out with a slotted spoon, and remove to a side dish. Discard any that do not open. Break off the empty half shells and discard.

5 Spread some of the puréed tomatoes on the pizza base, leaving the rim uncovered. Dot evenly with the prawns and squid rings and tentacles. Sprinkle with the garlic, parsley, salt and pepper, and olive oil.

6 Bake for about 8 minutes. Remove from the oven, and add the mussels in the half shells. Return to the oven and bake for 7–10 minutes more, or until the crust is golden. Serve the seafood pizza immediately.

Mussel & Leek Pizzettes

Serve these tasty seafood pizzettes with a crisp green or mixed salad for a light summer lunch.

Serves 4

INGREDIENTS
450 g/1 lb fresh mussels
120 ml/4 fl oz/½ cup dry white wine
4 x 13 cm/5 in round pizza bases
15 ml/1 tbsp olive oil
50 g/2 oz Gruyère cheese
50 g/2 oz Mozzarella cheese
2 small leeks
salt and freshly ground
   black pepper

1 Preheat the oven to 220°C/425°F/ Gas 7. Place the mussels in a bowl of cold water to soak, and scrub well. Remove the beards, scrape off any barnacles and discard any mussels that are open or have broken shells.

VARIATION: Frozen or canned mussels can also be used, but will not have the same flavour and texture. Make sure you defrost the mussels properly.

2 Place the mussels in a pan. Pour over the wine, bring to the boil, cover and cook over a high heat, shaking the pan occasionally, for 5–10 minutes, until the mussels have opened.

3 Drain off the cooking liquid. Remove the mussels from their shells, discarding any that remain closed. Leave to cool.

4 Place the pizza bases well apart on two greased baking sheets, then push up the dough edges to form a thin rim. Brush the pizza bases with the oil. Grate the cheeses and sprinkle half evenly over the bases.

5 Thinly slice the leeks, then scatter over the cheese. Bake for 10 minutes, then remove from the oven.

6 Arrange the mussels on top. Season and sprinkle over the remaining cheese. Bake for a further 5–10 minutes, until crisp and golden and the cheese is bubbling. Serve immediately.

Prawn & Sun-dried Tomato Pizzettes

Sun-dried tomatoes make an excellent topping for pizzas.

Serves 4

INGREDIENTS
1 quantity Basic or Superquick Pizza Dough
30 ml/2 tbsp Chilli Oil
75 g/3 oz/¾ cup grated Mozzarella cheese
1 garlic clove, chopped
½ small red onion, thinly sliced
4–6 pieces sun-dried tomatoes,
   thinly sliced
115 g/4 oz cooked prawns, peeled
30 ml/2 tbsp chopped fresh basil
salt and freshly ground black pepper
shredded fresh basil leaves, to garnish

1 Preheat the oven to 220°C/425°F/ Gas 7. Divide the dough into eight equal pieces.

2 Roll out each one on a lightly floured surface to a small oval about 5 mm/¼ in thick. Place well apart on two greased baking sheets. Prick all over with a fork.

3 Brush the pizza bases with 15 ml/ 1 tbsp of the chilli oil and top with the grated Mozzarella cheese, leaving a 1 cm/½ in border.

4 Divide the garlic, onion, sun-dried tomatoes, prawns and basil among the pizza bases. Season and drizzle over the remaining chilli oil. Bake for 8–10 minutes, until crisp and golden. Garnish with shredded basil leaves and serve immediately.

Crab & Parmesan Calzonelli

If preferred, you can use prawns instead of crab in these miniature calzone.

Makes 10–12

INGREDIENTS
1 quantity Basic or Superquick Pizza Dough
115 g/4 oz mixed prepared crab meat,
   thawed if frozen
15 ml/1 tbsp double cream
30 ml/2 tbsp freshly grated Parmesan cheese
30 ml/2 tbsp chopped fresh parsley
1 garlic clove, crushed
salt and freshly ground black pepper
fresh parsley sprigs, to garnish

1 Preheat the oven to 200°C/400°F/ Gas 6. Roll out the dough on a lightly floured surface to 3 mm/⅛ in thick. Using a 7.5 cm/3 in plain round cutter stamp out 10–12 circles.

2 In a bowl mix together the crab meat, double cream, grated Parmesan, chopped fresh parsley, crushed garlic, salt and freshly ground black pepper.

3 Spoon a little of the filling on to one half of each circle. Dampen the edges with water and fold over to completely enclose the filling.

4 Seal the edges by pressing with a fork. Place well apart on two greased baking sheets. Bake for 10–15 minutes, until golden brown and crisp. Garnish with parsley sprigs and serve immediately.

Chicken, Shiitake Mushroom & Coriander

The addition of shiitake mushrooms adds an earthy flavour to this colourful pizza, while fresh red chilli adds a hint of spiciness.

Serves 3–4

INGREDIENTS
45 ml/3 tbsp olive oil
350 g/12 oz chicken breast fillets, skinned and cut into thin strips
1 bunch spring onions, sliced
1 fresh red chilli, seeded and chopped
1 red pepper, seeded and cut into thin strips
75 g/3 oz fresh shiitake mushrooms, sliced
45–60 ml/3–4 tbsp chopped fresh coriander
1 pizza base, 25–30 cm/10–12 in diameter
15 ml/1 tbsp Chilli Oil
150 g/5 oz Mozzarella cheese
salt and freshly ground black pepper

1 Preheat the oven to 220°C/425°F/ Gas 7. Heat 30 ml/2 tbsp of the olive oil in a wok or large frying pan.

2 Add the chicken, spring onions, chilli, pepper and mushrooms and stir-fry over a high heat for 2–3 minutes. Do not overcook.

3 Season to taste with salt and pepper. Pour off any excess oil, then set aside the chicken mixture to cool. Stir the fresh coriander into the chicken mixture.

4 Brush the pizza base with the chilli oil. Spread the chicken mixture and drizzle over the remaining olive oil.

COOK'S TIP: For the chicken mixture, cook the meat until firm but slightly pink within or it will overcook in the oven.

5 Grate the Mozzarella and sprinkle over. Bake for 15–20 minutes, until crisp and golden and the topping is bubbling. Serve immediately.

American Hot

This ever-popular pizza is spiced with green chillies and the topping includes slices of pepperoni.

Serves 2–3

INGREDIENTS
1 pizza base, 25–30 cm/10–12 in diameter
15 ml/1 tbsp olive oil
115 g/4 oz can peeled and chopped green
   chillies in brine, drained
1 quantity Tomato Sauce
75 g/3 oz sliced pepperoni
6 black olives
15 ml/1 tbsp chopped
   fresh oregano
115 g/4 oz/1 cup grated
   Mozzarella cheese
fresh oregano leaves,
   to garnish

1 Preheat the oven to 220°C/425°F/ Gas 7. Brush the pizza base with the olive oil.

2 Stir the green chillies into the tomato sauce, and spread the mixture evenly over the pizza base.

3 Scatter the pepperoni slices over the tomato sauce and chilli mixture.

4 Halve the olives lengthways, remove and discard the stones. Scatter the olive halves over the pepperoni, with the chopped oregano.

VARIATION: You can make this pizza as hot as you like. For a really fiery version, use fresh red or green chillies, seeded and cut into slices, in place of the chillies in brine. You could also substitute chorizo, which is even spicier, for the pepperoni.

5 Sprinkle over the grated Mozzarella and bake for 15–20 minutes, until the pizza is crisp and golden.

6 Garnish with fresh oregano leaves and serve immediately.

Caramelized Onion, Salami & Black Olive

The sweetness of the caramelized onion is offset by the salty olives and herbs in the pizza base and the sprinkling of Parmesan to finish.

Serves 4

INGREDIENTS
675 g/1½ lb red onions
60 ml/4 tbsp olive oil
12 black olives
1 quantity Basic or Superquick
    Pizza Dough
5 ml/1 tsp dried *herbes de Provence*
6–8 slices Italian salami, quartered
30–45 ml/2–3 tbsp freshly grated
    Parmesan cheese
freshly ground
    black pepper

1 Preheat the oven to 220°C/425°F/ Gas 7. Thinly slice the onions.

2 Heat 30 ml/2 tbsp of the oil in a pan and add the onions. Cover and cook gently for 15–20 minutes, stirring occasionally, until the onions are soft and very lightly coloured. Leave to cool.

3 Cut the olives in half lengthways, remove and discard the stones. Finely chop the olives.

4 Knead the dough on a lightly floured surface, adding the black olives and *herbes de Provence*. Roll out the dough and use to line a 30 x 18 cm/ 12 x 7 in Swiss roll tin. Push up the dough edges to make a thin rim and brush with half the remaining oil.

5 Spoon half the onions evenly over the base, then top with the quartered salami slices and the remaining onions.

6 Grind over plenty of black pepper and drizzle over the remaining oil. Bake for 15–20 minutes, until crisp and golden. Remove from the oven and sprinkle over the freshly grated Parmesan to serve.

Pancetta, Leek & Smoked Mozzarella

Smoked Mozzarella with its brownish smoky-flavoured skin, pancetta and leeks make this an extremely tasty and easy-to-prepare pizza.

Serves 4

INGREDIENTS
30 ml/2 tbsp freshly grated
  Parmesan cheese
1 quantity Basic or Superquick
  Pizza Dough
30 ml/2 tbsp olive oil
2 medium leeks, trimmed
8–12 slices pancetta
150 g/5 oz smoked Mozzarella cheese
freshly ground black pepper

1 Preheat the oven to 220°C/425°F/ Gas 7. Dust the work surface with the Parmesan, then knead into the dough.

2 Divide the dough into four pieces and roll out each one to a 13 cm/5 in circle. Place well apart on two greased baking sheets, then push up the edges to make a thin rim. Brush the bases with 15 ml/1 tbsp of the oil.

3 Thinly slice the leeks. Arrange the pancetta and leeks evenly over the four pizza bases.

4 Grate the smoked Mozzarella and sprinkle over. Drizzle over the remaining oil and season with pepper. Bake for 15–20 minutes, until crisp and golden. Serve immediately.

Prosciutto, Mushroom & Artichoke

Here is a pizza full of rich and varied flavours. For a delicious variation, use mixed cultivated mushrooms.

Serves 2–3

INGREDIENTS
4 bottled artichoke hearts in oil, drained
60 ml/4 tbsp olive oil
1 bunch spring onions, chopped
225 g/8 oz/3¼ cups sliced mushrooms
2 garlic cloves, chopped
1 pizza base, 25–30 cm/10–12 in diameter
8 slices prosciutto
60 ml/4 tbsp freshly grated Parmesan cheese
salt and freshly ground black pepper
fresh thyme sprigs, to garnish

1 Preheat the oven to 220°C/425°F/ Gas 7. Slice the artichokes.

2 Heat 30 ml/2 tbsp of the oil in a frying pan. Add the spring onions, mushrooms and garlic and fry over a moderate heat until all the juices have evaporated. Season with salt and pepper and leave to cool.

3 Brush the pizza base with half the remaining oil. Arrange the prosciutto, mushrooms and artichoke hearts on top.

4 Sprinkle over the Parmesan, then drizzle over the remaining oil and season. Bake for 15–20 minutes. Garnish with thyme sprigs and serve immediately.

Calzone

A calzone is a pizza made from a round or a rectangular-shaped base, folded over to enclose its filling. It can be eaten hot or cold.

Serves 4

INGREDIENTS
2 quantities Basic Pizza Dough
350 g/12 oz/1½ cups ricotta cheese
175 g/6 oz/1 cup cooked ham, cut into
  small dice
6 medium tomatoes, peeled, seeded
  and diced
8 fresh basil leaves, torn into pieces
175 g/6 oz/1½ cups Mozzarella cheese,
  cut into small dice
60 ml/4 tbsp freshly grated
  Parmesan cheese
salt and freshly ground
  black pepper
olive oil, for brushing

1 Preheat the oven to 240°C/475°F/ Gas 9. Divide the dough into four balls. Roll each ball out into a flat circle about 5 mm/¼ in thick.

2 Combine all the remaining ingredients except the oil in a bowl, and mix well. Season to taste.

3 Divide the filling among the four circles of dough, placing it on half of each circle and allowing a border of 2 cm/¾ in all around.

4 Fold the other half of the circle over. Crimp the edges of the dough together with your fingers to seal.

COOK'S TIP: The calzone is a speciality of Naples. Calzone means "trouser leg" in Italian. This pizza was so named because it resembled a leg of the baggy trousers worn by Neapolitan men in the 18th and 19th centuries.

5 Brush the calzone tops lightly with olive oil. Place them on lightly oiled baking sheets. Bake for about 15–20 minutes, or until the tops are golden brown and the dough is puffed.

Chilli Beef

Minced beef, red kidney beans and smoky cheese combined with oregano, cumin and chillies give this pizza a Mexican character.

Serves 4

INGREDIENTS
30 ml/2 tbsp olive oil
1 red onion, finely chopped
1 garlic clove, crushed
½ red pepper, seeded and finely chopped
175 g/6 oz/1½ cups lean minced beef
2.5 ml/½ tsp ground cumin
2 fresh red chillies, seeded and chopped
115 g/4 oz (drained weight) canned
   red kidney beans
1 quantity Basic or Superquick Pizza Dough
1 quantity Tomato Sauce
15 ml/1 tbsp chopped fresh oregano
50 g/2 oz/½ cup grated Mozzarella cheese
75 g/3 oz/¾ cup grated oak-smoked
   Cheddar cheese
salt and freshly ground black pepper

2 Add the cumin and chillies and continue to cook, stirring, for about 5 minutes. Add the beans and seasoning to taste.

3 Knead the dough on a lightly floured surface, roll out and use to line a 30 x 18 cm/12 x 7 in greased Swiss roll tin. Push up the dough edges to make a rim.

1 Preheat the oven to 220°C/425°F/Gas 7. Heat 15 ml/1 tbsp of the oil in a frying pan. Add the onion, garlic and red pepper and gently fry until soft. Increase the heat, add the beef and brown well, stirring constantly.

4 Spread the tomato sauce evenly over the pizza base.

5 Spoon over the beef and beans mixture into an even layer, then scatter over the oregano.

6 Sprinkle over the cheeses and bake for 15–20 minutes, until crisp and golden. Serve immediately.

COOK'S TIP: This beef sauce, before the beans are added, can be prepared in advance and kept for up to 3 days in the fridge.

Spring Vegetable & Pine Nut

This colourful pizza is packed with delicious vegetables. You can vary the ingredients according to availability.

Serves 2–3

INGREDIENTS
1 pizza base, 25–30 cm/10–12 in diameter
45 ml/3 tbsp Garlic Oil
1 quantity Tomato Sauce
4 spring onions
2 courgettes
1 leek
115 g/4 oz asparagus tips
15 ml/1 tbsp chopped fresh oregano
30 ml/2 tbsp pine nuts
50 g/2 oz/½ cup grated Mozzarella cheese
30 ml/2 tbsp freshly grated
   Parmesan cheese
freshly ground black pepper

1 Preheat the oven to 220°C/425°F/ Gas 7. Brush the pizza base with 15 ml/1 tbsp of the garlic oil, then spread over the tomato sauce.

2 Slice the spring onions, courgettes, leek and asparagus tips.

3 Heat half the remaining garlic oil in a frying pan and stir-fry the vegetables for 3–5 minutes.

4 Arrange the vegetables in an even layer over the tomato sauce.

5 Sprinkle the chopped fresh oregano and the pine nuts over the pizza.

COOK'S TIP: Prepare spring onions by first trimming off the outer skin. Then chop all the white and some of the green stems.

6 Mix together the Mozzarella and Parmesan and sprinkle over the pizza. Drizzle over the remaining garlic oil and season generously with pepper. Bake for 15–20 minutes, until crisp and golden. Serve immediately.

Mushroom & Pesto

This is a mouth-watering Mediterranean-style pizza.

Serves 4

INGREDIENTS
25 g/1 oz/¾ cup fresh basil
25 g/1 oz/¼ cup pine nuts
40 g/1½ oz Parmesan cheese, thinly sliced
105 ml/7 tbsp olive oil
50 g/2 oz/1 cup dried porcini mushrooms
2 onions, thinly sliced
225 g/8 oz/3¼ cups chestnut
 mushrooms, sliced
1 pizza base, 25–30 cm/10–12 in diameter
salt and freshly ground black pepper

1 First make the pesto topping. Place the basil, pine nuts, Parmesan and 75 ml/5 tbsp of the olive oil in a blender or food processor and process to make a smooth paste. Set aside.

2 Soak the dried mushrooms in hot water for 20 minutes.

3 Fry the onions in the remaining olive oil for 3–4 minutes until beginning to colour. Add the chestnut mushrooms and fry for 2 minutes. Stir in the drained porcini mushrooms and season lightly.

4 Preheat the oven to 220°C/425°F/ Gas 7. Lightly grease a large baking sheet and place the pizza base on it.

5 Spread the pesto mixture to within 1 cm/½ in of the edge. Spread the mushroom mixture on top. Bake the pizza for 35–40 minutes, until risen and golden. Serve immediately.

Sicilian

This robust-flavoured pizza is topped with roasted aubergine and cheese.

Serves 2

INGREDIENTS
1 small aubergine, cut into thin rounds
30 ml/2 tbsp olive oil
½ quantity Basic or Superquick
   Pizza Dough
½ quantity Tomato Sauce
175 g/6 oz Mozzarella cheese, sliced
50 g/2 oz/½ cup stoned
   black olives
15 ml/1 tbsp capers, drained
60 ml/4 tbsp grated Pecorino cheese
salt and freshly ground black pepper

1 Preheat the oven to 200°C/400°F/ Gas 6. Place the aubergine rounds on an oiled baking sheet and brush with the olive oil.

2 Bake for 10–15 minutes, turning once, until browned and tender. Remove the aubergine slices and drain on kitchen paper.

3 Increase the oven temperature to 220°C/425°F/Gas 7. Roll out the pizza dough to two 20 cm/8 in rounds. Transfer to baking sheets and spread with the tomato sauce.

4 Pile the aubergine slices on top of the tomato sauce and cover with the Mozzarella. Dot with the black olives and capers. Sprinkle the Pecorino liberally over the top, and season with plenty of salt and pepper. Bake for 15–20 minutes, until the crust on each pizza is golden. Serve immediately.

Courgette, Sweetcorn & Plum Tomato Wholewheat Pizza

This tasty wholewheat pizza can be served hot or cold with a mixed bean salad and fresh crusty bread or baked potatoes.

Serves 6

INGREDIENTS
225 g/8 oz/2 cups plain wholemeal flour
pinch of salt
10 ml/2 tsp baking powder
50 g/2 oz/4 tbsp margarine
150 ml/¼ pint/⅔ cup milk
30 ml/2 tbsp tomato purée
10 ml/2 tsp dried *herbes de Provence*
10 ml/2 tsp olive oil
1 onion, sliced
1 garlic clove, crushed
2 small courgettes, sliced
115 g/4 oz/1½ cups sliced mushrooms
115 g/4 oz/⅔ cup frozen
    sweetcorn kernels
2 plum tomatoes, sliced
50 g/2 oz/½ cup finely grated
    Red Leicester cheese
50 g/2 oz/½ cup finely grated
    Mozzarella cheese
salt and freshly ground
    black pepper
fresh basil sprigs, to garnish

1 Preheat the oven to 220°C/425°F/ Gas 7. Line a baking sheet with non-stick baking paper. Put the flour, salt and baking powder in a bowl and rub the margarine lightly into the flour until the mixture has the texture of fine breadcrumbs.

2 Add enough milk, a little at a time, to form a soft dough and knead lightly. Roll the dough out on a lightly floured surface, to a circle about 25 cm/10 in diameter.

3 Place the dough on the prepared baking sheet and make the edges slightly thicker than the centre. Spread the tomato purée over the base and sprinkle the dried herbs on top.

4 Heat the oil in a frying pan, add the onion, garlic, courgettes and mushrooms and cook gently for 10 minutes, stirring occasionally.

5 Spread the vegetable mixture over the pizza base and sprinkle over the sweetcorn and seasoning. Arrange the tomato slices on top.

6 Mix together the cheeses and sprinkle over the pizza. Bake for 25–30 minutes, until cooked and golden brown. Serve the pizza hot or cold in slices, garnished with basil sprigs.

COOK'S TIP: This pizza is ideal for freezing in portions or slices. Freeze for up to 3 months.

Roasted Vegetable & Goat's Cheese

Here is a pizza that incorporates the smoky flavours of oven-roasted vegetables with the distinctive taste of goat's cheese.

Serves 3

INGREDIENTS

1 aubergine, cut into thick chunks
2 courgettes, halved and sliced lengthways
1 red pepper, quartered and seeded
1 yellow pepper, quartered and seeded
1 small red onion, cut into wedges
90 ml/6 tbsp Garlic Oil
1 pizza base, 25–30 cm/10–12 in diameter
400 g/14 oz can chopped tomatoes, drained well.
115 g/4 oz goat's cheese (with rind)
15 ml/1 tbsp chopped fresh thyme
freshly ground black pepper
ready-made green olive tapenade, to serve

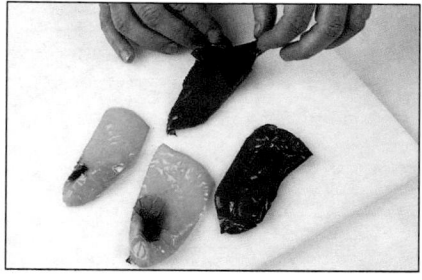

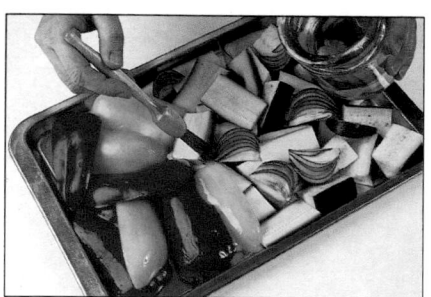

1 Preheat the oven to 220°C/425°F/ Gas 7. Place the aubergine, courgettes, peppers and onion in a large roasting tin. Brush with 60 ml/4 tbsp of the garlic oil. Roast for about 30 minutes, turning the peppers and courgettes halfway through cooking.

2 Remove the peppers from the oven and transfer to a plastic bag, using tongs. Seal the top and set aside. When they are cool enough to handle, peel off the skins and cut the flesh into thick strips.

3 Brush the pizza's base with half the remaining garlic oil and spread the drained tomatoes over.

4 Arrange the roasted vegetables evenly on top of the pizza base.

5 Cut the goat's cheese into chunks and arrange them on top of the vegetables. Scatter over the thyme.

6 Drizzle over the remaining garlic oil and season with pepper. Bake for 15–20 minutes, until crisp and golden. Spoon the tapenade over, to serve.

New Potato & Garlic

A strongly-flavoured pizza which makes the most of the new season's potatoes.

Serves 2–3

INGREDIENTS
350 g/12 oz new potatoes
45 ml/3 tbsp olive oil
2 garlic cloves, crushed
1 pizza base, 25–30 cm/10–12 in diameter
1 red onion, thinly sliced
150 g/5 oz/1¼ cups grated smoked
   Mozzarella cheese
10 ml/2 tsp chopped fresh rosemary
salt and freshly ground black pepper
30 ml/2 tbsp freshly grated Parmesan cheese,
   to garnish

1 Preheat the oven to 220°C/425°F/
Gas 7. Cook the potatoes in boiling
salted water for 5 minutes. Drain well.
When cool, peel and slice thinly.

2 Heat 30 ml/2 tbsp of the oil in a
frying pan. Add the sliced potatoes and
garlic and fry for 5–8 minutes, until
brown and tender.

3 Brush the pizza base with the
remaining oil. Scatter over the onion,
then arrange the potatoes on top.

4 Sprinkle over the Mozzarella and
rosemary. Grind over plenty of pepper
and bake for 15–20 minutes, until
crisp and golden. Remove from the
oven and sprinkle over the Parmesan
to serve.

Butternut Squash & Sage

An unusual combination of sweet and savoury ingredients.

Serves 4

INGREDIENTS
15 g/½ oz/1 tbsp butter
30 ml/2 tbsp olive oil
2 shallots, finely chopped
1 butternut squash, peeled, seeded and
   cubed, about 450 g/1 lb prepared weight
16 sage leaves
3 quantities Basic or Superquick Pizza Dough
1½ quantities Tomato Sauce
115 g/4 oz sliced Mozzarella cheese
115 g/4 oz/½ cup firm goat's cheese
salt and freshly ground black pepper

1 Preheat the oven to 200°C/400°F/
Gas 6. Heat the butter and oil in a
roasting tin and add the shallots, squash
and half the sage leaves.

2 Toss the vegetables to coat and roast
for 15–20 minutes, until tender.

3 Raise the oven temperature to
220°C/425°F/Gas 7. Divide the pizza
dough into four equal pieces and roll
out into 20 cm/8 in rounds. Oil two
large baking sheets.

4 Place each round on a baking sheet
and spread with tomato sauce. Spoon
the squash and shallot mixture over
the top.

5 Cover with Mozzarella and crumbled
goat's cheese. Garnish with sage leaves,
season and bake for 15–20 minutes,
until the cheese has melted and the
crust on each pizza has turned golden.

Smoked Salmon Pizzettes

Sophisticated mini pizzas topped with smoked salmon, crème fraîche and lumpfish roe make an extra special party canapé.

Makes 10–12

INGREDIENTS
1 quantity Basic or Superquick
    Pizza Dough
15 ml/1 tbsp snipped fresh chives
15 ml/1 tbsp olive oil
75–115 g/3–4 oz smoked salmon,
    cut into strips
60 ml/4 tbsp crème fraîche
30 ml/2 tbsp black lumpfish roe
fresh chives, to garnish

1 Preheat the oven to 200°C/400°F/ Gas 6. Knead the dough gently, adding the snipped chives until evenly mixed.

2 Roll out the dough on a lightly floured surface to about 3 mm/⅛ in thick. Using a 7.5 cm/3 in plain round cutter, stamp out 10–12 circles.

3 Place the bases well apart on two greased baking sheets, prick all over with a fork, then brush with the oil. Bake for 10–15 minutes until the bases are crisp and golden.

4 Arrange the smoked salmon on top, then spoon on the crème fraîche. Spoon a tiny amount of lumpfish roe in the centre and garnish with chives. Serve immediately.

Mozzarella, Anchovy & Pesto

These delightful little pizzas combine the piquancy of olives and capers with anchovies and Mozzarella cheese.

Makes 24

INGREDIENTS
2 quantities Basic or Superquick
Pizza Dough
60 ml/4 tbsp olive oil
30 ml/2 tbsp red pesto
12 stoned black olives
75 g/3 oz Mozzarella cheese, cubed
50 g/2 oz (drained weight) sun-dried
tomatoes in oil, chopped
30–45 ml/2–3 tbsp capers, drained
50 g/2 oz can anchovy fillets, drained and
roughly chopped
30 ml/2 tbsp freshly grated Parmesan cheese
fresh parsley sprigs, to garnish

1 Preheat the oven to 220°C/425°F/Gas 7.

2 Roll out the dough on a lightly floured surface to about 3 mm/⅛ in thick. Using a 5 cm/2 in plain round cutter, stamp out 24 rounds. Place the rounds on two greased baking sheets.

3 Brush the bases with 30 ml/2 tbsp of the oil, then spread over the pesto.

4 Cut the olives into quarters lengthways, then scatter over the bases with the Mozzarella, sun-dried tomatoes, capers and anchovies.

5 Sprinkle over the Parmesan and drizzle over the remaining oil. Bake for 8–10 minutes, until crisp and golden. Transfer to a warm platter, garnish with parsley sprigs and serve.

Smoked Chicken, Yellow Pepper and Sun-dried Tomato Pizzettes

These ingredients complement each other perfectly and make a really delicious and colourful topping.

Serves 4

INGREDIENTS
1 quantity Basic or Superquick
   Pizza Dough
45 ml/3 tbsp olive oil
60 ml/4 tbsp sun-dried tomato paste
2 yellow peppers, seeded and cut into
   thin strips
175 g/6 oz sliced smoked chicken or
   turkey, chopped
150 g/5 oz/1¼ cups Mozzarella
   cheese, cubed
30 ml/2 tbsp chopped fresh basil
salt and freshly ground
   black pepper

1 Preheat the oven to 220°C/425°F/ Gas 7. Divide the prepared dough into four equal pieces and roll out each one on a lightly floured surface to a 13 cm/ 5 in circle.

2 Place well apart on two greased baking sheets, then push up the dough edges to make a thin rim. Brush with 15 ml/1 tbsp of the oil.

3 Brush the pizza bases generously with the sun-dried tomato paste and set aside.

4 Stir-fry the peppers in half the remaining oil for 3–4 minutes.

5 Arrange the chicken and peppers on top of the sun-dried tomato paste.

VARIATION: For a vegetarian pizza with a similar smoky taste, omit the chicken, roast the yellow peppers and remove the skins before using, and replace the Mozzarella with Bavarian smoked cheese.

6 Scatter over the Mozzarella and basil. Season with salt and pepper.

7 Drizzle over the remaining oil and bake for 15–20 minutes, until crisp and golden. Serve immediately.

Spinach & Ricotta Panzerotti

These make great party food to serve with drinks or as tasty appetizers for a crowd of hungry guests.

Makes 20–24

INGREDIENTS
115 g/4 oz frozen chopped spinach, thawed and squeezed dry
50 g/2 oz/¼ cup ricotta cheese
50 g/2 oz/⅔ cup freshly grated Parmesan
generous pinch freshly grated nutmeg
2 quantities Basic or Superquick Pizza Dough
1 egg white, lightly beaten
vegetable oil, for deep-frying
salt and freshly ground black pepper

1 Place the spinach, ricotta, Parmesan, nutmeg and seasoning in a bowl and beat until smooth.

COOK'S TIP: Do serve these as soon as possible after frying, as they will become much less appetizing if left to cool.

2 Roll out the dough on a lightly floured surface to about 3 mm/⅛ in thick. Using a 7.5 cm/3 in plain round cutter stamp out 20–24 circles.

3 Spread a teaspoon of spinach mixture over one half of each circle.

4 Brush the edges of the dough with a little egg white.

5 Fold the dough over the filling and press the edges firmly together to seal.

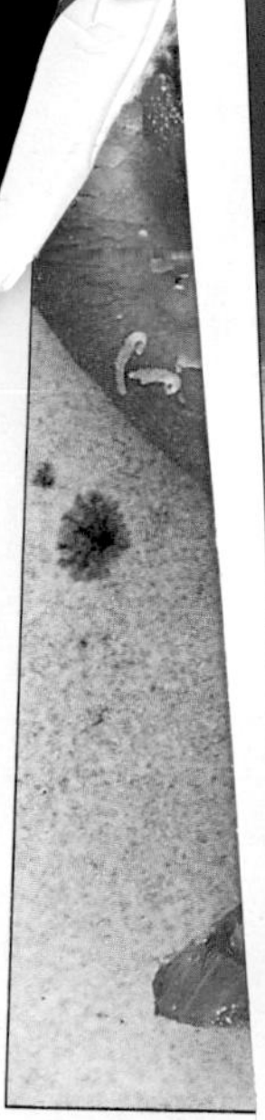

5 Arrange ha
over each base
the Mozzarella
Drizzle with t
each one in the
shelf for 12–15
the edge of the
brown and the t
and bubbling.

6 Heat the oil in a large, heavy-based pan or deep-fat fryer to 180°C/350°F. Deep-fry the panzerotti, a few at a time, for 2–3 minutes, until golden. Drain thoroughly on kitchen paper and serve immediately.

Sp Feta, Pimiento
Pi: & Pine Nut Pizzettes

These   Delight your guests with these tempting small pizzas. Substitute goat

Makes cheese for the feta if you prefer.

Makes 24

INGREL
45–60 m

INGREDIENTS
2 onions,
2 quantities Basic or Superquick
2 garlic c.
    Pizza Dough
225 g/8 o:
flour for rolling dough
225 g/8 o:
60 ml/4 tbsp olive oil, plus extra for greasing
225 g/8 oz
30 ml/2 tbsp ready-made black
spicy sa
    olive tapenade
5 ml/1 tsp
175 g/6 oz feta cheese
5 ml/1 tsp
1 large canned pimiento, drained
115 g/4 oz
30 ml/2 tbsp chopped fresh thyme
drained a
30 ml/2 tbsp pine nuts
450 g/1 lb
freshly ground black pepper
well drair
fresh thyme sprigs, to garnish
225 g/8 oz/2
60 ml/4 tbsp
stoned black
fresh basil le
strips of red
FOR THE DO
cornmeal, for
2 quantities B
Pizza Dougl
30 ml/1 tbsp v

2 Brush a thin layer of the black olive tapenade on each oval and crumble over the feta cheese.

3 Cut the pimiento into thin strips and pile evenly on top of the cheese.

1 Preheat the oven to 220°C/425°F/ Gas 7. Divide the pizza dough into 24 pieces and roll out each one on a lightly floured surface to a small oval, about 3 mm/⅛ in thick. Place well apart on greased baking sheets and prick all over with a fork. Brush with 30 ml/2 tbsp of the oil.

4 Sprinkle each one with thyme and pine nuts. Drizzle over the remaining oil and grind over plenty of pepper. Bake for 10–15 minutes, until crisp and golden. Garnish with thyme sprigs and serve immediately.

1 In a large,
oil over a me
onions and c
softened. Add
mushrooms a
more, until th
soften and col

This Paperback edition published by Hermes House
an imprint of
Anness Publishing Limited
Hermes House
88-89 Blackfriars Road
London SE1 8HA

A CIP catalogue record for this book is available from the British Library

© Anness Publishing Limited 2000

Publisher: Joanna Lorenz
Editor: Valerie Ferguson
Series Designer: Bobbie Colgate Stone
Designer: Andrew Heath
Production Controller: Joanna King

Recipes contributed by: Angela Boggiano,
Carla Capalbo, Jacqueline Clark, Shirley Gill,
Anne Sheasby, Elizabeth Wolf-Cohen,
Jeni Wright.

Photography: William Adams-Lingwood,
Karl Adamson, Joanna Farrow, Michelle Garrett,
Amanda Heywood, Janine Hosegood,
David Jordan.

1 3 5 7 9 10 8 6 4 2

Notes:
For all recipes, quantities are given in both metric
and imperial measures and, where appropriate,
measures are also given in standard cups
and spoons.
Follow one set, but not a mixture, because they
are not interchangeable.

Standard spoon and cup measures are level.

1 tsp = 5 ml   1 tbsp = 15 ml

1 cup = 250 ml/8 fl oz

Australian standard tablespoons are 20 ml.
Australian readers should use 3 tsp in place of
1 tbsp for measuring small quantities of gelatine,
cornflour, salt, etc.

Medium eggs are used unless otherwise stated.

Printed and bound in China